W9-BEX-765

For more than a dozen years, Mike Peyton has been known through the yachting press of many countries for his special brand of cartoon and also for articles. He lives on an Essex estuary with his wife and two daughters, from where he runs two ferro charter yachts, skippering the forty-foot *Lodestone* and having a watching brief on the thirty-five foot *Brimstone*. Whether in these home waters or those further away in which he sails, he tries to avoid cartoon situations—but with only partial success.

# COME SAILING AGAIN
# MIKE PEYTON

# Nautical

First published in Great Britain by
NAUTICAL PUBLISHING CO LTD
Lymington, Hampshire SO4 9BA

ISBN 0 245 52991 8

Filmset, printed and bound in
Great Britain by R. J. Acford Ltd,
Chichester, Sussex

# CONTENTS

# INTRODUCTION

This is my second sincere attempt to warn people
of the so-called joys of sailing and, although in all
fairness, I must give credit to my publishers for
helping me in my campaign, I have a vague feeling
that we may, in a manner of speaking, be in the
same boat. But, like the yachtsman and the bird
he had conned on board, we are not necessarily of
the same mind. They hope you will laugh again
at these cautionary drawings, whereas I know and
you know that although these incidents have not
actually happened to you, if you sail long enough
they will. But you will not be laughing then.

North Fambridge.                                    M.P.

# INFANTS IN THE CRADLE OF THE DEEP

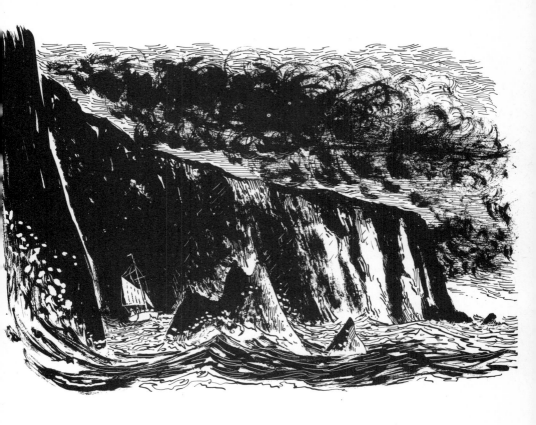

"*The Pilot just says 'A delightful anchorage in settled conditions'.*"

"*That red flasher is now reading: 'Toby Ales', John, and
    the fixed white: 'Ladies'.*"

"*They're lost too.*"

*"Just keep her jogging along while I have a recap."*

*"Go to sleep, dear, it's just car headlights leaving the pub."*

"*The last time I pulled this one he gybed all standing and broke his boom.*"

*"That Black Conical which put us spot on course, David . . ."*

*"Look, I was sitting in a bar with six Pernods inside me when I thought a quick dash back was a good idea."*

"*The tide must be stronger than I thought. We're north of
the South Goodwin light vessel.*"

"*They're more snobbish than the Royal Yacht Squadron.*"

"*There's a difference between spot-on and head-on.*"

"*Sometimes, Dave, I feel sailing is only a little better than work.*"

"*If it is any consolation, Humber, Thames, Dover, Wight are having 2 to 3 southerlies.*"

"*Well, if he isn't lost we are.*"

# HARD RACING CROPPERS

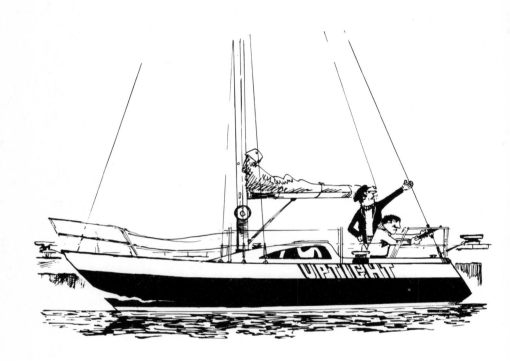

`` . . . It's still pretty slack.''

24

"*I'll give you three guesses which one we want.*"

*"Who bagged that bloody spinnaker?"*

"*Hughie, Hughie, where the hell are you? That spinnaker has twisted.*"

27

"*Permission to come on board, Skip.*"

*"Skip, Skip! Do something."*

"*I admit it's unusual, but he's flying no distress signals and what's more to the point we're leading our class.*"

# THE FEMALE OF THE SPECIES

"*I beg your pardon, Madam.*"

"*Are you coming in for your Christmas dinner, or shall I leave it in the oven?*"

32

"*I think Joan is finally getting interested. It was her who suggested I fit out early.*"

"*I'm sorry she tipped the paint over you: but after four years,
the night I start painting the kitchen you want a hand.*"

"*Of course I rowed back in the dinghy; how else?*"

*"Enjoy yourselves, boys."*

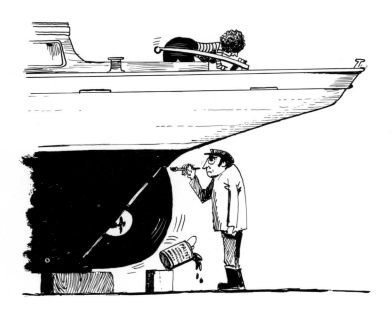

*"Darling."*

*"I'm so glad we agreed to paint it blue this year."*

"*I see he has his bird down this weekend.*"

"*It's John. He's sunk the boat! I will be interested to see how he transfers the blame to me.*"

# TOUCHING BOTTOM

*"I know I thought it a good idea then, but I'm sober now".*

*"John! John! Where are you? The water's coming back!"*

*"Thinking of getting rid of the old Silhouette, then?"*

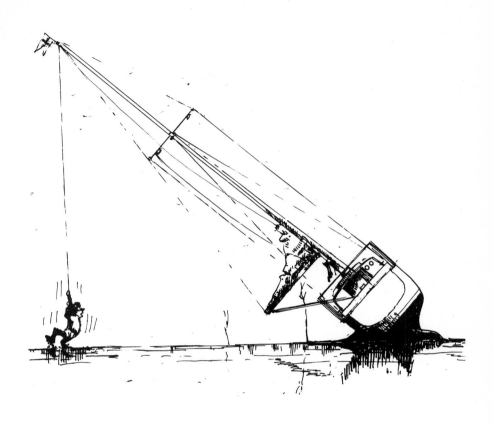

*"Daddy!"*

"*I admit we could be worse off, but not much, it's just gone low water.*"

"*I know the boat is designed to take the ground, but every weekend?*"

"*As you say, we've still got the dinghy.*"

*"Relax, I know this bit of water like the back of . . ."*

"*Naughty Doggie.*"

"*I costed it out: petrol, travelling time, yard bills . . .*"

# RELAX WE'VE STOPPED

*"Has no one told you that the days of sailing in are over?"*

*"Don't get excited darling, everything is under control."*

*"We brought Bounder along, we knew you wouldn't mind."*

"*One thing about bilge keelers: they take the ground in comfort.*"

*"And I'm selling her with a complete set of storm canvas."*

*"Ever noticed the tide always serves at two in the morning
when it is raining?"*

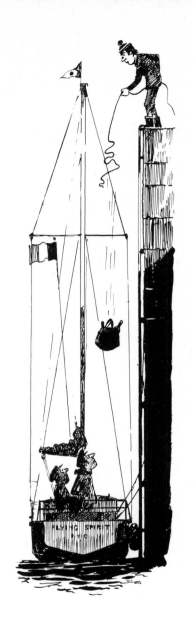

*"Duty free coming dow . . ."*

*"I'll not be a minute, dear, I'll just give a quick pump out."*

60

"*Lets start again, taking the standing part in your left hand,
form a bight with . . .*"

"*I say old boy, if you're off the little cutter that picked up
the end mooring, you can't leave her there.*"

"*Save work, back it right down to load the dinghy, that's
    what you said.*"

"*That swell seems to have taken off.*"

64

*"We're going ashore for the evening, old chap. Can we bring
you anything back?"*

"I generally give them an hour to get comfortable before I
wake them and tell them they can't lie here."

66

"*Darling, I think this is the gentleman whose dinghy you borrowed.*"

# DOWN BELOW

*"Escapism from what?"*

"*If that lot whistling past his ear doesn't wake him up,
nothing will.*"

"Put the purée into an earthenware casserole, with the juice
of the lemon and the hearts of three cooked artichokes,
sauté the liver . . ."

*"What's this in my boot?"*

*"Faeroes, South East Iceland . . ."*

# OVER THE BAR

"*One of the best runs ashore I have ever had, old chap.*"

*"He'll be back."*

"*Better take your 'Quells', dear, school's out.*"

"*If he says he's had a Nicholson 32 in his stocking again, I'll do him.*"

# LITTLE UPS
# AND DOWNS

*"I thought you said you had a forty horse diesel below . . . ?"*

"*Bloke hanging on to the bobstay, Fred, wants to know the name of your insurance.*"

*"Hold your course, John , we don't want to confuse him now."*

*"I'll never understand women, just before we left my wife said we were stupid."*

*"The tide's just turning, they'll lie comfortably then."*

82

*"Easy does it."*

*"It'll be good to get in, tie up and relax."*

"*And from the looks of it, they'll have damn all to declare, if we do get on board.*"

# WORKING ON IT

*"Fit a skin fitting, piece of cake, do it between tides easily,
that's what you said."*

"*That's me ready for the season.*"

"*Hold it Joe, what was the name of this mast?*"

"*Bert, there is a piece of brass with three holes in it been kicking around the cockpit for months, would you hand it down?*"

". . . *your left arm behind you, steady yourself on the exhaust
pipe, put your right arm forward and up a bit, feel about
and there's a burred nut . . .*"

*"Somehow, I don't feel the boat show is me."*

*"I see someone has frapped that tapping halyard for you."*

92

*"Sorry John, a bit of a slip up, but everything under control now."*

"*Relax chaps, it's clear, I can turn the shaft easily.*"

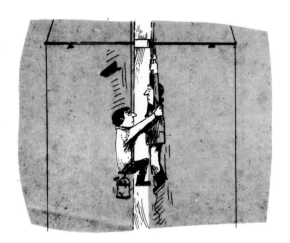